Let's Make Friends

By Janine Amos and Annabel Spenceley

Consultant Rachael Underwood

an imprint of
WINDMILL BOOKS
New York

Published in the United States by Alphabet Soup, an imprint of Windmill Books, LLC

Windmill Books
303 Park Avenue South
Suite #1280
New York, NY 10010

U.S. publication copyright © 2010 Evans Brothers Limited
First North American Edition

Library of Congress Cataloging-in-Publication Data

Amos, Janine
    Let's make friends. – 1st North American ed. / by Janine Amos and Annabel Spenceley.
        p.   cm. – (Best behavior)
    Contents: Splashing in puddles—Building a house.
    Summary: Two brief stories demonstrate how to make new friends at the park and during indoor activities.
    ISBN 978-1-60754-500-2 (lib.) – 978-1-60754-499-9 (pbk.)
978-1-60754-502-6 (6 pack)   4355   6330   9/10
    1. Friendship—Juvenile literature   2. Social interaction—Juvenile literature
[1. Friendship   2. Conduct of life]   I. Spenceley, Annabel   II. Title   III. Series
    177/.62—dc22

Manufactured in China

With thanks to: Megan and Sonia Sear, Olivia Varley, Kirsty and Connor Sweeney, Kellah-Monique Henry, Aman Jutla, and Moya Saunders.

Splashing in Puddles

Splash!
It's been raining.

4

Megan is jumping
in a puddle.

5

Megan sees a girl.

"Hey!" says Megan.
"You've got boots on too.
You can splash with me."

Olivia goes to the puddle.

She jumps with Megan.

Megan's mom smiles at them.
"You've made friends,"
she says.

Building a House

The children are
building a house.

Kellah is
watching.

Kellah pushes the blocks.

The house tumbles down.

"Don't do that!" shouts Moya. "Now we have to build it again."

How do you think
Moya feels?
How does Kellah feel?

Kellah walks away.

Bryony follows her.

"You seem unhappy,"
says Bryony.

"Did you want to play?"

Kellah nods her head.

"If you'd like to join in,
you can," says Bryony.
"Tell the children what
you want."

23

"You come too,"
says Kellah.

They go over to the blocks.

"Can I play, please?" Kellah
says to the children.

"Put some blocks on
the roof," Moya tells her.

Kellah builds the roof with Moya.

They work together.

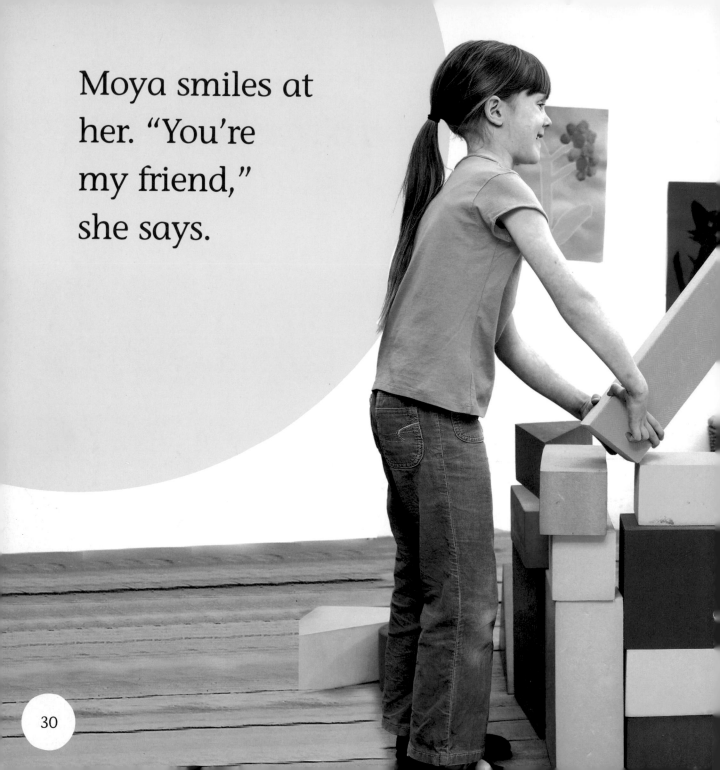

Moya smiles at her. "You're my friend," she says.

How does Kellah
feel now?

oks.com

FOR FURTHER READING

INFORMATION BOOKS
Greive, Bradley Trevor. *Friends to the End: The True Value of Friendship*. Riverside, NJ: Andrews McMeel Publishing, 2004.

Krasny Brown, Laurie. *How to Be a Friend: A Guide to Making Friends and Keeping Them*. Boston: Little, Brown Young Readers, 2001.

FICTION
Niemann, Christoph. *The Pet Dragon: A Story about Adventure, Friendship, and Chinese Characters*. New York: HarperCollins, 2008.

AUTHOR BIO

Janine Amos has worked in publishing as an editor and author, and as a lecturer in education. Her interests are in personal growth and raising self-esteem, and she works with educators, child psychologists, and specialists in mediation. She has written more than fifty books for children. Many of her titles deal with first-time experiences and emotional health issues such as bullying, death, and divorce.

You can find more great fiction and nonfiction from Windmill Books at windmillbo